Pool Maintenance Log Book

Name:

Address:

Email:

Phone No:

Weekly Maintenance Checklists for you to Complete. Helping you to Keep your Pool Clean, Safe and Problem Free.

Regular inspections and maintenance will ensure that your Swimming Pool is in optimum condition. You can deal with any problems as they arise - instead of letting problems escalate into expensive repair bills.

Name / Location of Pool:

Today's Date:

Number of Days since Last Check:

Pool Maintenance Check List	Tick Box Yes/No	Additional Notes / Comments
Check Filters:		
Check Pumps:		
Check Water Temperature:		Record Water Temperature:
Check Water Level:		Amount of Water Added:
Water Test: PH: (ideal 7.4 – 7.6)		PH Level:
Water Test: Chlorine: (ideal 1.5 – 2.5)		Chlorine Level: If applicable, record how much Chlorine Added:
Clean and Check Skimmer Baskets:		

Brush Sides:		
Leaf Skimming:		
Vacuum Pool:		
Check your Stock of Pool Chemicals:		Chemicals / Items to Purchase:
Check your First Aid Supplies:		Items to Purchase:
Check Pool Side – any fences or gates:		If applicable, list maintenance required:
Overall Water Clarity:		

Further Notes / Observations:

_____
_____
_____
_____
_____

Name / Location of Pool:

Today's Date:

Number of Days since Last Check:

Pool Maintenance Check List	Tick Box Yes/No	Additional Notes / Comments
Check Filters:		
Check Pumps:		
Check Water Temperature:		Record Water Temperature:
Check Water Level:		Amount of Water Added:
Water Test: PH: (ideal 7.4 – 7.6)		PH Level:
Water Test: Chlorine: (ideal 1.5 – 2.5)		Chlorine Level: If applicable, record how much Chlorine Added:
Clean and Check Skimmer Baskets:		

Brush Sides:		
Leaf Skimming:		
Vacuum Pool:		
Check your Stock of Pool Chemicals:		Chemicals / Items to Purchase:
Check your First Aid Supplies:		Items to Purchase:
Check Pool Side – any fences or gates:		If applicable, list maintenance required:
Overall Water Clarity:		

Further Notes / Observations:

_____
_____
_____
_____
_____

Name / Location of Pool:

Today's Date:

Number of Days since Last Check:

Pool Maintenance Check List	Tick Box Yes/No	Additional Notes / Comments
Check Filters:		
Check Pumps:		
Check Water Temperature:		Record Water Temperature:
Check Water Level:		Amount of Water Added:
Water Test: PH: (ideal 7.4 – 7.6)		PH Level:
Water Test: Chlorine: (ideal 1.5 – 2.5)		Chlorine Level: If applicable, record how much Chlorine Added:
Clean and Check Skimmer Baskets:		

Brush Sides:		
Leaf Skimming:		
Vacuum Pool:		
Check your Stock of Pool Chemicals:		Chemicals / Items to Purchase:
Check your First Aid Supplies:		Items to Purchase:
Check Pool Side – any fences or gates:		If applicable, list maintenance required:
Overall Water Clarity:		

Further Notes / Observations:

_____
_____
_____
_____
_____

Name / Location of Pool:

Today's Date:

Number of Days since Last Check:

Pool Maintenance Check List	Tick Box Yes/No	Additional Notes / Comments
Check Filters:		
Check Pumps:		
Check Water Temperature:		Record Water Temperature:
Check Water Level:		Amount of Water Added:
Water Test: PH: (ideal 7.4 – 7.6)		PH Level:
Water Test: Chlorine: (ideal 1.5 – 2.5)		Chlorine Level: If applicable, record how much Chlorine Added:
Clean and Check Skimmer Baskets:		

Brush Sides:		
Leaf Skimming:		
Vacuum Pool:		
Check your Stock of Pool Chemicals:		Chemicals / Items to Purchase:
Check your First Aid Supplies:		Items to Purchase:
Check Pool Side – any fences or gates:		If applicable, list maintenance required:
Overall Water Clarity:		

Further Notes / Observations:

_____
_____
_____
_____
_____

Name / Location of Pool:

Today's Date:

Number of Days since Last Check:

Pool Maintenance Check List	Tick Box Yes/No	Additional Notes / Comments
Check Filters:		
Check Pumps:		
Check Water Temperature:		Record Water Temperature:
Check Water Level:		Amount of Water Added:
Water Test: PH: (ideal 7.4 – 7.6)		PH Level:
Water Test: Chlorine: (ideal 1.5 – 2.5)		Chlorine Level: If applicable, record how much Chlorine Added:
Clean and Check Skimmer Baskets:		

Brush Sides:		
Leaf Skimming:		
Vacuum Pool:		
Check your Stock of Pool Chemicals:		Chemicals / Items to Purchase:
Check your First Aid Supplies:		Items to Purchase:
Check Pool Side – any fences or gates:		If applicable, list maintenance required:
Overall Water Clarity:		

Further Notes / Observations:

_____

_____

_____

_____

_____

Name / Location of Pool:

Today's Date:

Number of Days since Last Check:

Pool Maintenance Check List	Tick Box Yes/No	Additional Notes / Comments
Check Filters:		
Check Pumps:		
Check Water Temperature:		Record Water Temperature:
Check Water Level:		Amount of Water Added:
Water Test: PH: (ideal 7.4 – 7.6)		PH Level:
Water Test: Chlorine: (ideal 1.5 – 2.5)		Chlorine Level: If applicable, record how much Chlorine Added:
Clean and Check Skimmer Baskets:		

Brush Sides:		
Leaf Skimming:		
Vacuum Pool:		
Check your Stock of Pool Chemicals:		Chemicals / Items to Purchase:
Check your First Aid Supplies:		Items to Purchase:
Check Pool Side – any fences or gates:		If applicable, list maintenance required:
Overall Water Clarity:		

Further Notes / Observations:

_____

_____

_____

_____

_____

Name / Location of Pool:

Today's Date:

Number of Days since Last Check:

Pool Maintenance Check List	Tick Box Yes/No	Additional Notes / Comments
Check Filters:		
Check Pumps:		
Check Water Temperature:		Record Water Temperature:
Check Water Level:		Amount of Water Added:
Water Test: PH: (ideal 7.4 – 7.6)		PH Level:
Water Test: Chlorine: (ideal 1.5 – 2.5)		Chlorine Level: If applicable, record how much Chlorine Added:
Clean and Check Skimmer Baskets:		

Brush Sides:		
Leaf Skimming:		
Vacuum Pool:		
Check your Stock of Pool Chemicals:		Chemicals / Items to Purchase:
Check your First Aid Supplies:		Items to Purchase:
Check Pool Side – any fences or gates:		If applicable, list maintenance required:
Overall Water Clarity:		

Further Notes / Observations:

_____
_____
_____
_____
_____

Name / Location of Pool:

Today's Date:

Number of Days since Last Check:

Pool Maintenance Check List	Tick Box Yes/No	Additional Notes / Comments
Check Filters:		
Check Pumps:		
Check Water Temperature:		Record Water Temperature:
Check Water Level:		Amount of Water Added:
Water Test: PH: (ideal 7.4 – 7.6)		PH Level:
Water Test: Chlorine: (ideal 1.5 – 2.5)		Chlorine Level: If applicable, record how much Chlorine Added:
Clean and Check Skimmer Baskets:		

Brush Sides:		
Leaf Skimming:		
Vacuum Pool:		
Check your Stock of Pool Chemicals:		Chemicals / Items to Purchase:
Check your First Aid Supplies:		Items to Purchase:
Check Pool Side – any fences or gates:		If applicable, list maintenance required:
Overall Water Clarity:		

Further Notes / Observations:

_____

_____

_____

_____

_____

Name / Location of Pool:

Today's Date:

Number of Days since Last Check:

Pool Maintenance Check List	Tick Box Yes/No	Additional Notes / Comments
Check Filters:		
Check Pumps:		
Check Water Temperature:		Record Water Temperature:
Check Water Level:		Amount of Water Added:
Water Test: PH: (ideal 7.4 – 7.6)		PH Level:
Water Test: Chlorine: (ideal 1.5 – 2.5)		Chlorine Level: If applicable, record how much Chlorine Added:
Clean and Check Skimmer Baskets:		

Brush Sides:		
Leaf Skimming:		
Vacuum Pool:		
Check your Stock of Pool Chemicals:		Chemicals / Items to Purchase:
Check your First Aid Supplies:		Items to Purchase:
Check Pool Side – any fences or gates:		If applicable, list maintenance required:
Overall Water Clarity:		

Further Notes / Observations:

_____

_____

_____

_____

_____

Name / Location of Pool:

Today's Date:

Number of Days since Last Check:

Pool Maintenance Check List	Tick Box Yes/No	Additional Notes / Comments
Check Filters:		
Check Pumps:		
Check Water Temperature:		Record Water Temperature:
Check Water Level:		Amount of Water Added:
Water Test: PH: (ideal 7.4 – 7.6)		PH Level:
Water Test: Chlorine: (ideal 1.5 – 2.5)		Chlorine Level: If applicable, record how much Chlorine Added:
Clean and Check Skimmer Baskets:		

Brush Sides:		
Leaf Skimming:		
Vacuum Pool:		
Check your Stock of Pool Chemicals:		Chemicals / Items to Purchase:
Check your First Aid Supplies:		Items to Purchase:
Check Pool Side – any fences or gates:		If applicable, list maintenance required:
Overall Water Clarity:		

Further Notes / Observations:

_____
_____
_____
_____
_____

Name / Location of Pool:

Today's Date:

Number of Days since Last Check:

Pool Maintenance Check List	Tick Box Yes/No	Additional Notes / Comments
Check Filters:		
Check Pumps:		
Check Water Temperature:		Record Water Temperature:
Check Water Level:		Amount of Water Added:
Water Test: PH: (ideal 7.4 – 7.6)		PH Level:
Water Test: Chlorine: (ideal 1.5 – 2.5)		Chlorine Level: If applicable, record how much Chlorine Added:
Clean and Check Skimmer Baskets:		

Brush Sides:		
Leaf Skimming:		
Vacuum Pool:		
Check your Stock of Pool Chemicals:		Chemicals / Items to Purchase:
Check your First Aid Supplies:		Items to Purchase:
Check Pool Side – any fences or gates:		If applicable, list maintenance required:
Overall Water Clarity:		

Further Notes / Observations:

_____

_____

_____

_____

_____

Name / Location of Pool:

Today's Date:

Number of Days since Last Check:

Pool Maintenance Check List	Tick Box Yes/No	Additional Notes / Comments
Check Filters:		
Check Pumps:		
Check Water Temperature:		Record Water Temperature:
Check Water Level:		Amount of Water Added:
Water Test: PH: (ideal 7.4 – 7.6)		PH Level:
Water Test: Chlorine: (ideal 1.5 – 2.5)		Chlorine Level: If applicable, record how much Chlorine Added:
Clean and Check Skimmer Baskets:		

Brush Sides:		
Leaf Skimming:		
Vacuum Pool:		
Check your Stock of Pool Chemicals:		Chemicals / Items to Purchase:
Check your First Aid Supplies:		Items to Purchase:
Check Pool Side – any fences or gates:		If applicable, list maintenance required:
Overall Water Clarity:		

Further Notes / Observations:

_____

_____

_____

_____

_____

Name / Location of Pool:

Today's Date:

Number of Days since Last Check:

Pool Maintenance Check List	Tick Box Yes/No	Additional Notes / Comments
Check Filters:		
Check Pumps:		
Check Water Temperature:		Record Water Temperature:
Check Water Level:		Amount of Water Added:
Water Test: PH: (ideal 7.4 – 7.6)		PH Level:
Water Test: Chlorine: (ideal 1.5 – 2.5)		Chlorine Level: If applicable, record how much Chlorine Added:
Clean and Check Skimmer Baskets:		

Brush Sides:		
Leaf Skimming:		
Vacuum Pool:		
Check your Stock of Pool Chemicals:		Chemicals / Items to Purchase:
Check your First Aid Supplies:		Items to Purchase:
Check Pool Side – any fences or gates:		If applicable, list maintenance required:
Overall Water Clarity:		

Further Notes / Observations:

_____

_____

_____

_____

_____

Name / Location of Pool:

Today's Date:

Number of Days since Last Check:

Pool Maintenance Check List	Tick Box Yes/No	Additional Notes / Comments
Check Filters:		
Check Pumps:		
Check Water Temperature:		Record Water Temperature:
Check Water Level:		Amount of Water Added:
Water Test: PH: (ideal 7.4 – 7.6)		PH Level:
Water Test: Chlorine: (ideal 1.5 – 2.5)		Chlorine Level: If applicable, record how much Chlorine Added:
Clean and Check Skimmer Baskets:		

Brush Sides:		
Leaf Skimming:		
Vacuum Pool:		
Check your Stock of Pool Chemicals:		Chemicals / Items to Purchase:
Check your First Aid Supplies:		Items to Purchase:
Check Pool Side – any fences or gates:		If applicable, list maintenance required:
Overall Water Clarity:		

Further Notes / Observations:

_____

_____

_____

_____

_____

Name / Location of Pool:

Today's Date:

Number of Days since Last Check:

Pool Maintenance Check List	Tick Box Yes/No	Additional Notes / Comments
Check Filters:		
Check Pumps:		
Check Water Temperature:		Record Water Temperature:
Check Water Level:		Amount of Water Added:
Water Test: PH: (ideal 7.4 – 7.6)		PH Level:
Water Test: Chlorine: (ideal 1.5 – 2.5)		Chlorine Level: If applicable, record how much Chlorine Added:
Clean and Check Skimmer Baskets:		

Brush Sides:		
Leaf Skimming:		
Vacuum Pool:		
Check your Stock of Pool Chemicals:		Chemicals / Items to Purchase:
Check your First Aid Supplies:		Items to Purchase:
Check Pool Side – any fences or gates:		If applicable, list maintenance required:
Overall Water Clarity:		

Further Notes / Observations:

_____

_____

_____

_____

_____

Name / Location of Pool:

Today's Date:

Number of Days since Last Check:

Pool Maintenance Check List	Tick Box Yes/No	Additional Notes / Comments
Check Filters:		
Check Pumps:		
Check Water Temperature:		Record Water Temperature:
Check Water Level:		Amount of Water Added:
Water Test: PH: (ideal 7.4 – 7.6)		PH Level:
Water Test: Chlorine: (ideal 1.5 – 2.5)		Chlorine Level: If applicable, record how much Chlorine Added:
Clean and Check Skimmer Baskets:		

Brush Sides:		
Leaf Skimming:		
Vacuum Pool:		
Check your Stock of Pool Chemicals:		Chemicals / Items to Purchase:
Check your First Aid Supplies:		Items to Purchase:
Check Pool Side – any fences or gates:		If applicable, list maintenance required:
Overall Water Clarity:		

Further Notes / Observations:

_____
_____
_____
_____
_____

Name / Location of Pool:

Today's Date:

Number of Days since Last Check:

Pool Maintenance Check List	Tick Box Yes/No	Additional Notes / Comments
Check Filters:		
Check Pumps:		
Check Water Temperature:		Record Water Temperature:
Check Water Level:		Amount of Water Added:
Water Test: PH: (ideal 7.4 – 7.6)		PH Level:
Water Test: Chlorine: (ideal 1.5 – 2.5)		Chlorine Level: If applicable, record how much Chlorine Added:
Clean and Check Skimmer Baskets:		

Brush Sides:		
Leaf Skimming:		
Vacuum Pool:		
Check your Stock of Pool Chemicals:		Chemicals / Items to Purchase:
Check your First Aid Supplies:		Items to Purchase:
Check Pool Side – any fences or gates:		If applicable, list maintenance required:
Overall Water Clarity:		

Further Notes / Observations:

_____
_____
_____
_____
_____

Name / Location of Pool:

Today's Date:

Number of Days since Last Check:

Pool Maintenance Check List	Tick Box Yes/No	Additional Notes / Comments
Check Filters:		
Check Pumps:		
Check Water Temperature:		Record Water Temperature:
Check Water Level:		Amount of Water Added:
Water Test: PH: (ideal 7.4 – 7.6)		PH Level:
Water Test: Chlorine: (ideal 1.5 – 2.5)		Chlorine Level: If applicable, record how much Chlorine Added:
Clean and Check Skimmer Baskets:		

Brush Sides:		
Leaf Skimming:		
Vacuum Pool:		
Check your Stock of Pool Chemicals:		Chemicals / Items to Purchase:
Check your First Aid Supplies:		Items to Purchase:
Check Pool Side – any fences or gates:		If applicable, list maintenance required:
Overall Water Clarity:		

Further Notes / Observations:

_____

_____

_____

_____

_____

Name / Location of Pool:

Today's Date:

Number of Days since Last Check:

Pool Maintenance Check List	Tick Box Yes/No	Additional Notes / Comments
Check Filters:		
Check Pumps:		
Check Water Temperature:		Record Water Temperature:
Check Water Level:		Amount of Water Added:
Water Test: PH: (ideal 7.4 – 7.6)		PH Level:
Water Test: Chlorine: (ideal 1.5 – 2.5)		Chlorine Level: If applicable, record how much Chlorine Added:
Clean and Check Skimmer Baskets:		

Brush Sides:		
Leaf Skimming:		
Vacuum Pool:		
Check your Stock of Pool Chemicals:		Chemicals / Items to Purchase:
Check your First Aid Supplies:		Items to Purchase:
Check Pool Side – any fences or gates:		If applicable, list maintenance required:
Overall Water Clarity:		

Further Notes / Observations:

_____
_____
_____
_____
_____

Name / Location of Pool:

Today's Date:

Number of Days since Last Check:

Pool Maintenance Check List	Tick Box Yes/No	Additional Notes / Comments
Check Filters:		
Check Pumps:		
Check Water Temperature:		Record Water Temperature:
Check Water Level:		Amount of Water Added:
Water Test: PH: (ideal 7.4 – 7.6)		PH Level:
Water Test: Chlorine: (ideal 1.5 – 2.5)		Chlorine Level: If applicable, record how much Chlorine Added:
Clean and Check Skimmer Baskets:		

Brush Sides:		
Leaf Skimming:		
Vacuum Pool:		
Check your Stock of Pool Chemicals:		Chemicals / Items to Purchase:
Check your First Aid Supplies:		Items to Purchase:
Check Pool Side – any fences or gates:		If applicable, list maintenance required:
Overall Water Clarity:		

Further Notes / Observations:

_____

_____

_____

_____

_____

Name / Location of Pool:

Today's Date:

Number of Days since Last Check:

Pool Maintenance Check List	Tick Box Yes/No	Additional Notes / Comments
Check Filters:		
Check Pumps:		
Check Water Temperature:		Record Water Temperature:
Check Water Level:		Amount of Water Added:
Water Test: PH: (ideal 7.4 – 7.6)		PH Level:
Water Test: Chlorine: (ideal 1.5 – 2.5)		Chlorine Level: If applicable, record how much Chlorine Added:
Clean and Check Skimmer Baskets:		

Brush Sides:		
Leaf Skimming:		
Vacuum Pool:		
Check your Stock of Pool Chemicals:		Chemicals / Items to Purchase:
Check your First Aid Supplies:		Items to Purchase:
Check Pool Side – any fences or gates:		If applicable, list maintenance required:
Overall Water Clarity:		

Further Notes / Observations:

_____

_____

_____

_____

_____

Name / Location of Pool:

Today's Date:

Number of Days since Last Check:

Pool Maintenance Check List	Tick Box Yes/No	Additional Notes / Comments
Check Filters:		
Check Pumps:		
Check Water Temperature:		Record Water Temperature:
Check Water Level:		Amount of Water Added:
Water Test: PH: (ideal 7.4 – 7.6)		PH Level:
Water Test: Chlorine: (ideal 1.5 – 2.5)		Chlorine Level: If applicable, record how much Chlorine Added:
Clean and Check Skimmer Baskets:		

Brush Sides:		
Leaf Skimming:		
Vacuum Pool:		
Check your Stock of Pool Chemicals:		Chemicals / Items to Purchase:
Check your First Aid Supplies:		Items to Purchase:
Check Pool Side – any fences or gates:		If applicable, list maintenance required:
Overall Water Clarity:		

Further Notes / Observations:

_____

_____

_____

_____

_____

Name / Location of Pool:

Today's Date:

Number of Days since Last Check:

Pool Maintenance Check List	Tick Box Yes/No	Additional Notes / Comments
Check Filters:		
Check Pumps:		
Check Water Temperature:		Record Water Temperature:
Check Water Level:		Amount of Water Added:
Water Test: PH: (ideal 7.4 – 7.6)		PH Level:
Water Test: Chlorine: (ideal 1.5 – 2.5)		Chlorine Level: If applicable, record how much Chlorine Added:
Clean and Check Skimmer Baskets:		

Brush Sides:		
Leaf Skimming:		
Vacuum Pool:		
Check your Stock of Pool Chemicals:		Chemicals / Items to Purchase:
Check your First Aid Supplies:		Items to Purchase:
Check Pool Side – any fences or gates:		If applicable, list maintenance required:
Overall Water Clarity:		

Further Notes / Observations:

_____
_____
_____
_____
_____

Name / Location of Pool:

Today's Date:

Number of Days since Last Check:

Pool Maintenance Check List	Tick Box Yes/No	Additional Notes / Comments
Check Filters:		
Check Pumps:		
Check Water Temperature:		Record Water Temperature:
Check Water Level:		Amount of Water Added:
Water Test: PH: (ideal 7.4 – 7.6)		PH Level:
Water Test: Chlorine: (ideal 1.5 – 2.5)		Chlorine Level: If applicable, record how much Chlorine Added:
Clean and Check Skimmer Baskets:		

Brush Sides:		
Leaf Skimming:		
Vacuum Pool:		
Check your Stock of Pool Chemicals:		Chemicals / Items to Purchase:
Check your First Aid Supplies:		Items to Purchase:
Check Pool Side – any fences or gates:		If applicable, list maintenance required:
Overall Water Clarity:		

Further Notes / Observations:

_____
_____
_____
_____
_____

Name / Location of Pool:

Today's Date:

Number of Days since Last Check:

Pool Maintenance Check List	Tick Box Yes/No	Additional Notes / Comments
Check Filters:		
Check Pumps:		
Check Water Temperature:		Record Water Temperature:
Check Water Level:		Amount of Water Added:
Water Test: PH: (ideal 7.4 – 7.6)		PH Level:
Water Test: Chlorine: (ideal 1.5 – 2.5)		Chlorine Level: If applicable, record how much Chlorine Added:
Clean and Check Skimmer Baskets:		

Brush Sides:		
Leaf Skimming:		
Vacuum Pool:		
Check your Stock of Pool Chemicals:		Chemicals / Items to Purchase:
Check your First Aid Supplies:		Items to Purchase:
Check Pool Side – any fences or gates:		If applicable, list maintenance required:
Overall Water Clarity:		

Further Notes / Observations:

_____
_____
_____
_____
_____

Name / Location of Pool:

Today's Date:

Number of Days since Last Check:

Pool Maintenance Check List	Tick Box Yes/No	Additional Notes / Comments
Check Filters:		
Check Pumps:		
Check Water Temperature:		Record Water Temperature:
Check Water Level:		Amount of Water Added:
Water Test: PH: (ideal 7.4 – 7.6)		PH Level:
Water Test: Chlorine: (ideal 1.5 – 2.5)		Chlorine Level: If applicable, record how much Chlorine Added:
Clean and Check Skimmer Baskets:		

Brush Sides:		
Leaf Skimming:		
Vacuum Pool:		
Check your Stock of Pool Chemicals:		Chemicals / Items to Purchase:
Check your First Aid Supplies:		Items to Purchase:
Check Pool Side – any fences or gates:		If applicable, list maintenance required:
Overall Water Clarity:		

Further Notes / Observations:

_____
_____
_____
_____
_____

Name / Location of Pool:

Today's Date:

Number of Days since Last Check:

Pool Maintenance Check List	Tick Box Yes/No	Additional Notes / Comments
Check Filters:		
Check Pumps:		
Check Water Temperature:		Record Water Temperature:
Check Water Level:		Amount of Water Added:
Water Test: PH: (ideal 7.4 – 7.6)		PH Level:
Water Test: Chlorine: (ideal 1.5 – 2.5)		Chlorine Level: If applicable, record how much Chlorine Added:
Clean and Check Skimmer Baskets:		

Brush Sides:		
Leaf Skimming:		
Vacuum Pool:		
Check your Stock of Pool Chemicals:		Chemicals / Items to Purchase:
Check your First Aid Supplies:		Items to Purchase:
Check Pool Side – any fences or gates:		If applicable, list maintenance required:
Overall Water Clarity:		

Further Notes / Observations:

_____

_____

_____

_____

_____

Name / Location of Pool:

Today's Date:

Number of Days since Last Check:

Pool Maintenance Check List	Tick Box Yes/No	Additional Notes / Comments
Check Filters:		
Check Pumps:		
Check Water Temperature:		Record Water Temperature:
Check Water Level:		Amount of Water Added:
Water Test: PH: (ideal 7.4 – 7.6)		PH Level:
Water Test: Chlorine: (ideal 1.5 – 2.5)		Chlorine Level: If applicable, record how much Chlorine Added:
Clean and Check Skimmer Baskets:		

Brush Sides:		
Leaf Skimming:		
Vacuum Pool:		
Check your Stock of Pool Chemicals:		Chemicals / Items to Purchase:
Check your First Aid Supplies:		Items to Purchase:
Check Pool Side – any fences or gates:		If applicable, list maintenance required:
Overall Water Clarity:		

Further Notes / Observations:

_____

_____

_____

_____

_____

Name / Location of Pool:

Today's Date:

Number of Days since Last Check:

Pool Maintenance Check List	Tick Box Yes/No	Additional Notes / Comments
Check Filters:		
Check Pumps:		
Check Water Temperature:		Record Water Temperature:
Check Water Level:		Amount of Water Added:
Water Test: PH: (ideal 7.4 – 7.6)		PH Level:
Water Test: Chlorine: (ideal 1.5 – 2.5)		Chlorine Level: If applicable, record how much Chlorine Added:
Clean and Check Skimmer Baskets:		

Brush Sides:		
Leaf Skimming:		
Vacuum Pool:		
Check your Stock of Pool Chemicals:		Chemicals / Items to Purchase:
Check your First Aid Supplies:		Items to Purchase:
Check Pool Side – any fences or gates:		If applicable, list maintenance required:
Overall Water Clarity:		

Further Notes / Observations:

_____

_____

_____

_____

_____

Name / Location of Pool:

Today's Date:

Number of Days since Last Check:

Pool Maintenance Check List	Tick Box Yes/No	Additional Notes / Comments
Check Filters:		
Check Pumps:		
Check Water Temperature:		Record Water Temperature:
Check Water Level:		Amount of Water Added:
Water Test: PH: (ideal 7.4 – 7.6)		PH Level:
Water Test: Chlorine: (ideal 1.5 – 2.5)		Chlorine Level: If applicable, record how much Chlorine Added:
Clean and Check Skimmer Baskets:		

Brush Sides:		
Leaf Skimming:		
Vacuum Pool:		
Check your Stock of Pool Chemicals:		Chemicals / Items to Purchase:
Check your First Aid Supplies:		Items to Purchase:
Check Pool Side – any fences or gates:		If applicable, list maintenance required:
Overall Water Clarity:		

Further Notes / Observations:

_____

_____

_____

_____

_____

Name / Location of Pool:

Today's Date:

Number of Days since Last Check:

Pool Maintenance Check List	Tick Box Yes/No	Additional Notes / Comments
Check Filters:		
Check Pumps:		
Check Water Temperature:		Record Water Temperature:
Check Water Level:		Amount of Water Added:
Water Test: PH: (ideal 7.4 – 7.6)		PH Level:
Water Test: Chlorine: (ideal 1.5 – 2.5)		Chlorine Level: If applicable, record how much Chlorine Added:
Clean and Check Skimmer Baskets:		

Brush Sides:		
Leaf Skimming:		
Vacuum Pool:		
Check your Stock of Pool Chemicals:		Chemicals / Items to Purchase:
Check your First Aid Supplies:		Items to Purchase:
Check Pool Side – any fences or gates:		If applicable, list maintenance required:
Overall Water Clarity:		

Further Notes / Observations:

_____
_____
_____
_____
_____

Name / Location of Pool:

Today's Date:

Number of Days since Last Check:

Pool Maintenance Check List	Tick Box Yes/No	Additional Notes / Comments
Check Filters:		
Check Pumps:		
Check Water Temperature:		Record Water Temperature:
Check Water Level:		Amount of Water Added:
Water Test: PH: (ideal 7.4 – 7.6)		PH Level:
Water Test: Chlorine: (ideal 1.5 – 2.5)		Chlorine Level: If applicable, record how much Chlorine Added:
Clean and Check Skimmer Baskets:		

Brush Sides:		
Leaf Skimming:		
Vacuum Pool:		
Check your Stock of Pool Chemicals:		Chemicals / Items to Purchase:
Check your First Aid Supplies:		Items to Purchase:
Check Pool Side – any fences or gates:		If applicable, list maintenance required:
Overall Water Clarity:		

Further Notes / Observations:

_____

_____

_____

_____

Name / Location of Pool:

Today's Date:

Number of Days since Last Check:

Pool Maintenance Check List	Tick Box Yes/No	Additional Notes / Comments
Check Filters:		
Check Pumps:		
Check Water Temperature:		Record Water Temperature:
Check Water Level:		Amount of Water Added:
Water Test: PH: (ideal 7.4 – 7.6)		PH Level:
Water Test: Chlorine: (ideal 1.5 – 2.5)		Chlorine Level: If applicable, record how much Chlorine Added:
Clean and Check Skimmer Baskets:		

Brush Sides:		
Leaf Skimming:		
Vacuum Pool:		
Check your Stock of Pool Chemicals:		Chemicals / Items to Purchase:
Check your First Aid Supplies:		Items to Purchase:
Check Pool Side – any fences or gates:		If applicable, list maintenance required:
Overall Water Clarity:		

Further Notes / Observations:

_____
_____
_____
_____
_____

Name / Location of Pool:

Today's Date:

Number of Days since Last Check:

Pool Maintenance Check List	Tick Box Yes/No	Additional Notes / Comments
Check Filters:		
Check Pumps:		
Check Water Temperature:		Record Water Temperature:
Check Water Level:		Amount of Water Added:
Water Test: PH: (ideal 7.4 – 7.6)		PH Level:
Water Test: Chlorine: (ideal 1.5 – 2.5)		Chlorine Level: If applicable, record how much Chlorine Added:
Clean and Check Skimmer Baskets:		

Brush Sides:		
Leaf Skimming:		
Vacuum Pool:		
Check your Stock of Pool Chemicals:		Chemicals / Items to Purchase:
Check your First Aid Supplies:		Items to Purchase:
Check Pool Side – any fences or gates:		If applicable, list maintenance required:
Overall Water Clarity:		

Further Notes / Observations:

_____

_____

_____

_____

_____

Name / Location of Pool:

Today's Date:

Number of Days since Last Check:

Pool Maintenance Check List	Tick Box Yes/No	Additional Notes / Comments
Check Filters:		
Check Pumps:		
Check Water Temperature:		Record Water Temperature:
Check Water Level:		Amount of Water Added:
Water Test: PH: (ideal 7.4 – 7.6)		PH Level:
Water Test: Chlorine: (ideal 1.5 – 2.5)		Chlorine Level: If applicable, record how much Chlorine Added:
Clean and Check Skimmer Baskets:		

Brush Sides:		
Leaf Skimming:		
Vacuum Pool:		
Check your Stock of Pool Chemicals:		Chemicals / Items to Purchase:
Check your First Aid Supplies:		Items to Purchase:
Check Pool Side – any fences or gates:		If applicable, list maintenance required:
Overall Water Clarity:		

Further Notes / Observations:

_____
_____
_____
_____
_____

Name / Location of Pool:

Today's Date:

Number of Days since Last Check:

Pool Maintenance Check List	Tick Box Yes/No	Additional Notes / Comments
Check Filters:		
Check Pumps:		
Check Water Temperature:		Record Water Temperature:
Check Water Level:		Amount of Water Added:
Water Test: PH: (ideal 7.4 – 7.6)		PH Level:
Water Test: Chlorine: (ideal 1.5 – 2.5)		Chlorine Level: If applicable, record how much Chlorine Added:
Clean and Check Skimmer Baskets:		

Brush Sides:		
Leaf Skimming:		
Vacuum Pool:		
Check your Stock of Pool Chemicals:		Chemicals / Items to Purchase:
Check your First Aid Supplies:		Items to Purchase:
Check Pool Side – any fences or gates:		If applicable, list maintenance required:
Overall Water Clarity:		

Further Notes / Observations:

_____
_____
_____
_____
_____

Name / Location of Pool:

Today's Date:

Number of Days since Last Check:

Pool Maintenance Check List	Tick Box Yes/No	Additional Notes / Comments
Check Filters:		
Check Pumps:		
Check Water Temperature:		Record Water Temperature:
Check Water Level:		Amount of Water Added:
Water Test: PH: (ideal 7.4 – 7.6)		PH Level:
Water Test: Chlorine: (ideal 1.5 – 2.5)		Chlorine Level: If applicable, record how much Chlorine Added:
Clean and Check Skimmer Baskets:		

Brush Sides:		
Leaf Skimming:		
Vacuum Pool:		
Check your Stock of Pool Chemicals:		Chemicals / Items to Purchase:
Check your First Aid Supplies:		Items to Purchase:
Check Pool Side – any fences or gates:		If applicable, list maintenance required:
Overall Water Clarity:		

Further Notes / Observations:

_____
_____
_____
_____
_____

Name / Location of Pool:

Today's Date:

Number of Days since Last Check:

Pool Maintenance Check List	Tick Box Yes/No	Additional Notes / Comments
Check Filters:		
Check Pumps:		
Check Water Temperature:		Record Water Temperature:
Check Water Level:		Amount of Water Added:
Water Test: PH: (ideal 7.4 – 7.6)		PH Level:
Water Test: Chlorine: (ideal 1.5 – 2.5)		Chlorine Level: If applicable, record how much Chlorine Added:
Clean and Check Skimmer Baskets:		

Brush Sides:		
Leaf Skimming:		
Vacuum Pool:		
Check your Stock of Pool Chemicals:		Chemicals / Items to Purchase:
Check your First Aid Supplies:		Items to Purchase:
Check Pool Side – any fences or gates:		If applicable, list maintenance required:
Overall Water Clarity:		

Further Notes / Observations:

_____
_____
_____
_____
_____

Name / Location of Pool:

Today's Date:

Number of Days since Last Check:

Pool Maintenance Check List	Tick Box Yes/No	Additional Notes / Comments
Check Filters:		
Check Pumps:		
Check Water Temperature:		Record Water Temperature:
Check Water Level:		Amount of Water Added:
Water Test: PH: (ideal 7.4 – 7.6)		PH Level:
Water Test: Chlorine: (ideal 1.5 – 2.5)		Chlorine Level: If applicable, record how much Chlorine Added:
Clean and Check Skimmer Baskets:		

Brush Sides:		
Leaf Skimming:		
Vacuum Pool:		
Check your Stock of Pool Chemicals:		Chemicals / Items to Purchase:
Check your First Aid Supplies:		Items to Purchase:
Check Pool Side – any fences or gates:		If applicable, list maintenance required:
Overall Water Clarity:		

Further Notes / Observations:

_____
_____
_____
_____
_____

Name / Location of Pool:

Today's Date:

Number of Days since Last Check:

Pool Maintenance Check List	Tick Box Yes/No	Additional Notes / Comments
Check Filters:		
Check Pumps:		
Check Water Temperature:		Record Water Temperature:
Check Water Level:		Amount of Water Added:
Water Test: PH: (ideal 7.4 – 7.6)		PH Level:
Water Test: Chlorine: (ideal 1.5 – 2.5)		Chlorine Level: If applicable, record how much Chlorine Added:
Clean and Check Skimmer Baskets:		

Brush Sides:		
Leaf Skimming:		
Vacuum Pool:		
Check your Stock of Pool Chemicals:		Chemicals / Items to Purchase:
Check your First Aid Supplies:		Items to Purchase:
Check Pool Side – any fences or gates:		If applicable, list maintenance required:
Overall Water Clarity:		

Further Notes / Observations:

_____
_____
_____
_____
_____

Name / Location of Pool:

Today's Date:

Number of Days since Last Check:

Pool Maintenance Check List	Tick Box Yes/No	Additional Notes / Comments
Check Filters:		
Check Pumps:		
Check Water Temperature:		Record Water Temperature:
Check Water Level:		Amount of Water Added:
Water Test: PH: (ideal 7.4 – 7.6)		PH Level:
Water Test: Chlorine: (ideal 1.5 – 2.5)		Chlorine Level: If applicable, record how much Chlorine Added:
Clean and Check Skimmer Baskets:		

Brush Sides:		
Leaf Skimming:		
Vacuum Pool:		
Check your Stock of Pool Chemicals:		Chemicals / Items to Purchase:
Check your First Aid Supplies:		Items to Purchase:
Check Pool Side – any fences or gates:		If applicable, list maintenance required:
Overall Water Clarity:		

Further Notes / Observations:

_____
_____
_____
_____
_____

Name / Location of Pool:

Today's Date:

Number of Days since Last Check:

Pool Maintenance Check List	Tick Box Yes/No	Additional Notes / Comments
Check Filters:		
Check Pumps:		
Check Water Temperature:		Record Water Temperature:
Check Water Level:		Amount of Water Added:
Water Test: PH: (ideal 7.4 – 7.6)		PH Level:
Water Test: Chlorine: (ideal 1.5 – 2.5)		Chlorine Level: If applicable, record how much Chlorine Added:
Clean and Check Skimmer Baskets:		

Brush Sides:		
Leaf Skimming:		
Vacuum Pool:		
Check your Stock of Pool Chemicals:		Chemicals / Items to Purchase:
Check your First Aid Supplies:		Items to Purchase:
Check Pool Side – any fences or gates:		If applicable, list maintenance required:
Overall Water Clarity:		

Further Notes / Observations:

_____
_____
_____
_____
_____

Name / Location of Pool:

Today's Date:

Number of Days since Last Check:

Pool Maintenance Check List	Tick Box Yes/No	Additional Notes / Comments
Check Filters:		
Check Pumps:		
Check Water Temperature:		Record Water Temperature:
Check Water Level:		Amount of Water Added:
Water Test: PH: (ideal 7.4 – 7.6)		PH Level:
Water Test: Chlorine: (ideal 1.5 – 2.5)		Chlorine Level: If applicable, record how much Chlorine Added:
Clean and Check Skimmer Baskets:		

Brush Sides:		
Leaf Skimming:		
Vacuum Pool:		
Check your Stock of Pool Chemicals:		Chemicals / Items to Purchase:
Check your First Aid Supplies:		Items to Purchase:
Check Pool Side – any fences or gates:		If applicable, list maintenance required:
Overall Water Clarity:		

Further Notes / Observations:

_____
_____
_____
_____
_____

Name / Location of Pool:

Today's Date:

Number of Days since Last Check:

Pool Maintenance Check List	Tick Box Yes/No	Additional Notes / Comments
Check Filters:		
Check Pumps:		
Check Water Temperature:		Record Water Temperature:
Check Water Level:		Amount of Water Added:
Water Test: PH: (ideal 7.4 – 7.6)		PH Level:
Water Test: Chlorine: (ideal 1.5 – 2.5)		Chlorine Level: If applicable, record how much Chlorine Added:
Clean and Check Skimmer Baskets:		

Brush Sides:		
Leaf Skimming:		
Vacuum Pool:		
Check your Stock of Pool Chemicals:		Chemicals / Items to Purchase:
Check your First Aid Supplies:		Items to Purchase:
Check Pool Side – any fences or gates:		If applicable, list maintenance required:
Overall Water Clarity:		

Further Notes / Observations:

_____
_____
_____
_____
_____

Name / Location of Pool:

Today's Date:

Number of Days since Last Check:

Pool Maintenance Check List	Tick Box Yes/No	Additional Notes / Comments
Check Filters:		
Check Pumps:		
Check Water Temperature:		Record Water Temperature:
Check Water Level:		Amount of Water Added:
Water Test: PH: (ideal 7.4 – 7.6)		PH Level:
Water Test: Chlorine: (ideal 1.5 – 2.5)		Chlorine Level: If applicable, record how much Chlorine Added:
Clean and Check Skimmer Baskets:		

Brush Sides:		
Leaf Skimming:		
Vacuum Pool:		
Check your Stock of Pool Chemicals:		Chemicals / Items to Purchase:
Check your First Aid Supplies:		Items to Purchase:
Check Pool Side – any fences or gates:		If applicable, list maintenance required:
Overall Water Clarity:		

Further Notes / Observations:

_____
_____
_____
_____
_____

<u>v</u> Name / Location of Pool:

Today's Date:

Number of Days since Last Check:

Pool Maintenance Check List	Tick Box Yes/No	Additional Notes / Comments
Check Filters:		
Check Pumps:		
Check Water Temperature:		Record Water Temperature:
Check Water Level:		Amount of Water Added:
Water Test: PH: (ideal 7.4 – 7.6)		PH Level:
Water Test: Chlorine: (ideal 1.5 – 2.5)		Chlorine Level: If applicable, record how much Chlorine Added:
Clean and Check Skimmer Baskets:		

Brush Sides:		
Leaf Skimming:		
Vacuum Pool:		
Check your Stock of Pool Chemicals:		Chemicals / Items to Purchase:
Check your First Aid Supplies:		Items to Purchase:
Check Pool Side – any fences or gates:		If applicable, list maintenance required:
Overall Water Clarity:		

Further Notes / Observations:

_____
_____
_____
_____
_____

Name / Location of Pool:

Today's Date:

Number of Days since Last Check:

Pool Maintenance Check List	Tick Box Yes/No	Additional Notes / Comments
Check Filters:		
Check Pumps:		
Check Water Temperature:		Record Water Temperature:
Check Water Level:		Amount of Water Added:
Water Test: PH: (ideal 7.4 – 7.6)		PH Level:
Water Test: Chlorine: (ideal 1.5 – 2.5)		Chlorine Level: If applicable, record how much Chlorine Added:
Clean and Check Skimmer Baskets:		

Brush Sides:		
Leaf Skimming:		
Vacuum Pool:		
Check your Stock of Pool Chemicals:		Chemicals / Items to Purchase:
Check your First Aid Supplies:		Items to Purchase:
Check Pool Side – any fences or gates:		If applicable, list maintenance required:
Overall Water Clarity:		

Further Notes / Observations:

_____
_____
_____
_____
_____

<u>v</u> Name / Location of Pool:

Today's Date:

Number of Days since Last Check:

Pool Maintenance Check List	Tick Box Yes/No	Additional Notes / Comments
Check Filters:		
Check Pumps:		
Check Water Temperature:		Record Water Temperature:
Check Water Level:		Amount of Water Added:
Water Test: PH: (ideal 7.4 – 7.6)		PH Level:
Water Test: Chlorine: (ideal 1.5 – 2.5)		Chlorine Level: If applicable, record how much Chlorine Added:
Clean and Check Skimmer Baskets:		

Brush Sides:		
Leaf Skimming:		
Vacuum Pool:		
Check your Stock of Pool Chemicals:		Chemicals / Items to Purchase:
Check your First Aid Supplies:		Items to Purchase:
Check Pool Side – any fences or gates:		If applicable, list maintenance required:
Overall Water Clarity:		

Further Notes / Observations:

_____
_____
_____
_____
_____

Name / Location of Pool:

Today's Date:

Number of Days since Last Check:

Pool Maintenance Check List	Tick Box Yes/No	Additional Notes / Comments
Check Filters:		
Check Pumps:		
Check Water Temperature:		Record Water Temperature:
Check Water Level:		Amount of Water Added:
Water Test: PH: (ideal 7.4 – 7.6)		PH Level:
Water Test: Chlorine: (ideal 1.5 – 2.5)		Chlorine Level: If applicable, record how much Chlorine Added:
Clean and Check Skimmer Baskets:		

Brush Sides:		
Leaf Skimming:		
Vacuum Pool:		
Check your Stock of Pool Chemicals:		Chemicals / Items to Purchase:
Check your First Aid Supplies:		Items to Purchase:
Check Pool Side – any fences or gates:		If applicable, list maintenance required:
Overall Water Clarity:		

Further Notes / Observations:

_____
_____
_____
_____
_____

Name / Location of Pool:

Today's Date:

Number of Days since Last Check:

Pool Maintenance Check List	Tick Box Yes/No	Additional Notes / Comments
Check Filters:		
Check Pumps:		
Check Water Temperature:		Record Water Temperature:
Check Water Level:		Amount of Water Added:
Water Test: PH: (ideal 7.4 – 7.6)		PH Level:
Water Test: Chlorine: (ideal 1.5 – 2.5)		Chlorine Level: If applicable, record how much Chlorine Added:
Clean and Check Skimmer Baskets:		

Brush Sides:		
Leaf Skimming:		
Vacuum Pool:		
Check your Stock of Pool Chemicals:		Chemicals / Items to Purchase:
Check your First Aid Supplies:		Items to Purchase:
Check Pool Side – any fences or gates:		If applicable, list maintenance required:
Overall Water Clarity:		

Further Notes / Observations:

_____
_____
_____
_____
_____

Name / Location of Pool:

Today's Date:

Number of Days since Last Check:

Pool Maintenance Check List	Tick Box Yes/No	Additional Notes / Comments
Check Filters:		
Check Pumps:		
Check Water Temperature:		Record Water Temperature:
Check Water Level:		Amount of Water Added:
Water Test: PH: (ideal 7.4 – 7.6)		PH Level:
Water Test: Chlorine: (ideal 1.5 – 2.5)		Chlorine Level: If applicable, record how much Chlorine Added:
Clean and Check Skimmer Baskets:		

Brush Sides:		
Leaf Skimming:		
Vacuum Pool:		
Check your Stock of Pool Chemicals:		Chemicals / Items to Purchase:
Check your First Aid Supplies:		Items to Purchase:
Check Pool Side – any fences or gates:		If applicable, list maintenance required:
Overall Water Clarity:		

Further Notes / Observations:

_____
_____
_____
_____
_____

Name / Location of Pool:

Today's Date:

Number of Days since Last Check:

Pool Maintenance Check List	Tick Box Yes/No	Additional Notes / Comments
Check Filters:		
Check Pumps:		
Check Water Temperature:		Record Water Temperature:
Check Water Level:		Amount of Water Added:
Water Test: PH: (ideal 7.4 – 7.6)		PH Level:
Water Test: Chlorine: (ideal 1.5 – 2.5)		Chlorine Level: If applicable, record how much Chlorine Added:
Clean and Check Skimmer Baskets:		

Brush Sides:		
Leaf Skimming:		
Vacuum Pool:		
Check your Stock of Pool Chemicals:		Chemicals / Items to Purchase:
Check your First Aid Supplies:		Items to Purchase:
Check Pool Side – any fences or gates:		If applicable, list maintenance required:
Overall Water Clarity:		

Further Notes / Observations:

_____
_____
_____
_____
_____

Further Notes:

Further Notes:

Further Notes:

Further Notes:

Further Notes:

Further Notes:

Further Notes:

Further Notes:

Further Notes:

Further Notes:

Thank you for using this Pool Maintenance Log Book. I sincerely hope that you have found it useful.

I appreciate your comments and any feedback. Please do take the time to leave a review. Simply find this journal on Amazon – 'Pool Maintenance Log Book' by Toni Patterson.

I look forward to hearing from you.

Made in the USA
Middletown, DE
07 September 2020